7/15 — 1/19
scircs

J

D0772407

Positive & Negative Numbers, Oh My!

Lisa Arias

Educational Media

rourkeeducationalmedia.com

Before Reading:

Building Academic Vocabulary and Background Knowledge

Before reading a book, it is important to tap into what your child or students already know about the topic. This will help them develop their vocabulary, increase their reading comprehension, and make connections across the curriculum.

1. *Look at the cover of the book. What will this book be about?*
2. *What do you already know about the topic?*
3. *Let's study the Table of Contents. What will you learn about in the book's chapters?*
4. *What would you like to learn about this topic? Do you think you might learn about it from this book? Why or why not?*
5. *Use a reading journal to write about your knowledge of this topic. Record what you already know about the topic and what you hope to learn about the topic.*
6. *Read the book.*
7. *In your reading journal, record what you learned about the topic and your response to the book.*
8. *After reading the book complete the activities below.*

Content Area Vocabulary
Read the list. What do these words mean?

absolute value

decimal

fraction

inequality

integer

natural numbers

negative numbers

quadrant

rational numbers

Roman Numerals

whole numbers

After Reading:

Comprehension and Extension Activity

After reading the book, work on the following questions with your child or students in order to check their level of reading comprehension and content mastery.

1. *How are rational and whole numbers different? (Asking questions)*
2. *What is the zero's purpose on a number line? (Summarize)*
3. *How are negative numbers part of your life? (Text to self connection)*
4. *What does absolute value mean? (Summarize)*
5. *Explain how quadrants relate to positive and negative numbers. (Summarize)*

Extension Activity

Positive and negative numbers affect us each day. Think about your day. Do you buy your lunch at school? Do you purchase a snack at a game? Make a chart on a piece of paper to track your expenses for a week. Start with how much money you have in your savings. Each time you buy something you decrease your savings. That means you subtract that amount. If you receive money from an allowance or special occasion you have gained money. You can add this amount to your savings total. At the end of the week how much money did you spend? How much did you earn?

Table of Contents

How Numbers Came to Be

The story of numbers began with **natural numbers** like 1, 2, and 3.

Next, zero became the hero and **whole numbers** came to be.

Before long, negatives needed a say,
so integers decided to come out to play.

4

But these numbers were not enough,
so **rational numbers** came in to do their stuff.

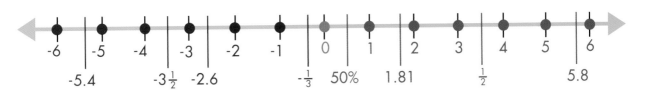

Next, we will look and see what integers mean to you and me.

Positive integers can be written with or without a positive sign.

3 or +3

Negative integers must be written with a negative sign.

−3

Positive and Negative Numbers

Opposites here, opposites there, opposites are everywhere.

Up

Down

Open

Closed

Hot

Cold

It's even true that numbers have opposites, too.
Zero separates positive and negative integers on the number line.

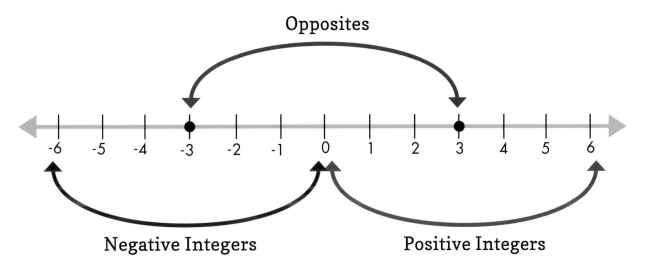

Opposite numbers are exactly the same distance from zero, but in opposite directions.

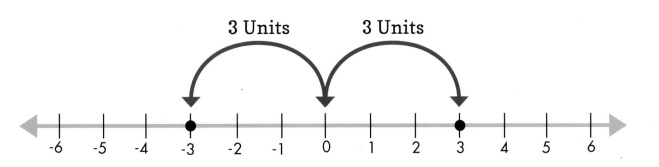

Find the opposite of each **integer**.

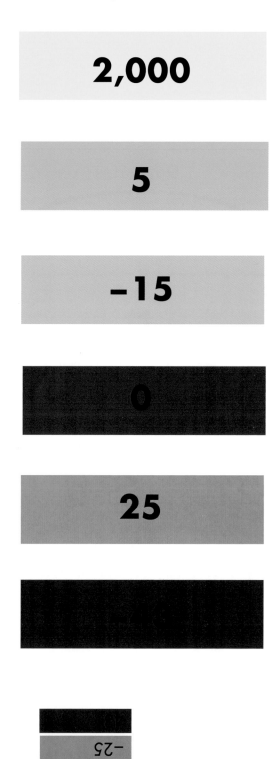

2,000

5

–15

0

25

Answers:
–2,000
–5
15

8

Check It Out!

Using this chart is really smart to help connect integers to real life situations.

Positive Integer	Negative Integer
Increase	Decrease
Over	Under
Above	Below
Ascend	Descend
Gain	Loss
Credit	Charge
Deposit	Withdraw
Receive	Owe

Examples:

Losing 12 pounds: −12

Earning $15: +15

Name the integer that represents each real world example.

Owe 5 hours

$25 loss

30 feet below sea level

Ascend 30,000 feet

Decrease 15 points

Withdraw $60

Increase 30 yards

Descend 10,000 feet

$1,000 Deposit

$50 Credit

Answers:

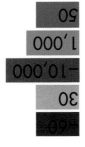

50
1,000
−10,000
30
−60

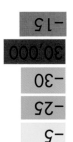

−15
30,000
−30
−25
−5

11

Absolute Value

Along with separating positive and negative integers, zero is key to finding the **absolute value** of any number you see.

The absolute value measures how far a number is from zero on a number line. Since you are only counting the distance, absolute values are always positive values.

Absolute value bars that surround the number being evaluated.

| |

Absolute Value Bars

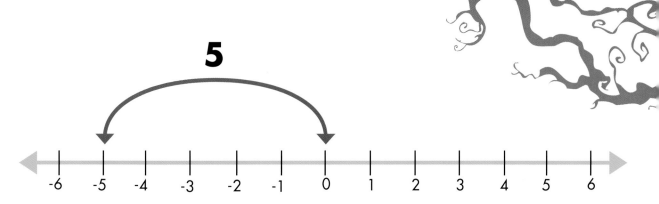

$$|-5| = 5$$

The absolute value of −5 is 5 because −5 is five units away from zero on the number line.

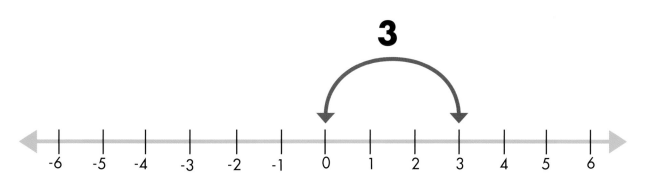

$$|3| = 3$$

The absolute value of 3 is 3 because 3 is three units away from zero on the number line.

Find the absolute value of each integer.

| 6 | | -6 |

| 0 | | -16 |

| 21 | | 31 |

| -19 | | 30 |

If a negative sign should appear outside of the absolute value bars, you are being asked for the opposite of the absolute value. Since absolute values are always positive, simply add a negative sign to your answer.

How do you evaluate the opposite of the absolute value of −21?

$$-\,|-21\,|$$

First, find the absolute value. $|-21| = 21$
Next, add a negative sign to your answer. −21
So, the opposite of the absolute value of −21 is −21.

$$-\,|-21\,| = -21$$

Find the opposite of the absolute values of each integer.

$$-\,|\,100\,|$$ $$-\,|\,25\,|$$

$$-\,|-1{,}200\,|$$ $$-\,|-4\,|$$

15

Compare and Order Numbers

Comparing numbers on a number line with **inequality** symbols works just fine.

Keep in mind:
Values increase as they move to the right.
Values decrease as they move to the left.

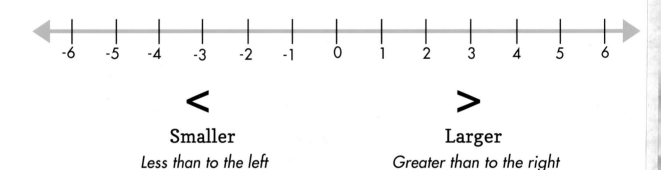

$$< $$
Smaller
Less than to the left

$$> $$
Larger
Greater than to the right

4 > 3

4 is greater than 3 because 4 is to the right of 3 on the number line.

–1 < 0

–1 is less than 0 because –1 is to the left of 0 on the number line.

Use < or > to compare each pair of integers.

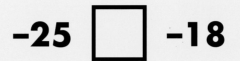

-25 ☐ -18

-71 ☐ -15

57 ☐ 35

-20 ☐ 20

-6 ☐ -7

To order from least to greatest, list the integers from left to right just as they appear on the number line.

7, 10, 2, 4, −8, −10

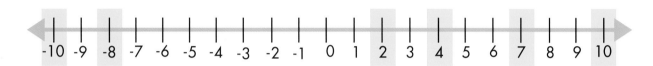

Order from least to greatest:

−10, −8, 2, 4, 7, 10

As the number line shows, each integer falls in order from left to right.

To order from greatest to least, list the integers from right to left just as they appear on the number line.

–1, –8, 6, –6, 0, 1

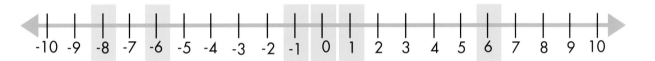

Order from greatest to least:

6, 1, 0, –1, –6, –8

As the number line shows, each integer falls in order from right to left.

Order the following integers from least to greatest.

-9, 7, 0, -5, 6, -2, 11, 5, -3

15, -7, -22, 36, -42, 0

9, -9, 105, -95, 47, -55, 33

24, -13, 43, -17, -6

Order the following integers from greatest to least.

30, –18, –26, 11, 0, –5, –23, 28

–22, –19, –6, 72, 3, 38

–45, 98, 3, –3, –63, –53, 13

16, –18, 10, 18, 11, –12, 34

Rational Numbers

Rational numbers are part of a whole and can be placed on number lines as fractions, percents, or decimals.

To graph fractions, split the number line between integers. Split the line into segments according to the denominator.

If you are graphing sixths, split the number line into six equal parts.

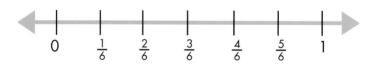

If you are graphing fifths, split the number line into five equal parts.

To graph decimals, split each section between integers into ten equal parts.

Keep in mind ordering rational numbers in different forms can put you in a bind.

Feel free to convert fractions and decimals into the same form, so your numbers will be uniform.

To convert fractions to decimals, divide the numerator by the denominator.

$$\frac{3}{4} = 3 \div 4 = 0.75$$

$$\frac{1}{5} = 1 \div 5 = 0.2$$

To convert decimals to fractions:
For decimals that are tenths, place over ten and simplify.

$$6.5 = 6\frac{5}{10} = 6\frac{1}{2}$$

For decimals in the hundredths, place over 100 and simplify.

$$1.25 = 1\frac{25}{100} = 1\frac{1}{4}$$

For decimals in the thousandths, place over 1,000 and simplify.

$$3.125 = 3\frac{125}{1,000} = 3\frac{1}{8}$$

Convert each **fraction** to a **decimal**.

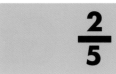

$$-1\frac{9}{10}$$

$$\frac{2}{5}$$

$$-\frac{7}{2}$$

$$\frac{2}{16}$$

Convert each decimal to a fraction in simplest form.

$$-0.4$$

$$2.55$$

$$0.64$$

$$-2.75$$

Four Quadrant Graphing

The coordinate plane is divided into four sections called quadrants. The four quadrants are there to help plot **negative numbers** from your ordered pair.

Each **quadrant** is labeled in **Roman Numerals**. Their order follows the shape of the letter C, quite conveniently.

Check It Out! 29

Thinking of the letter C is helpful to remember the quadrant order.

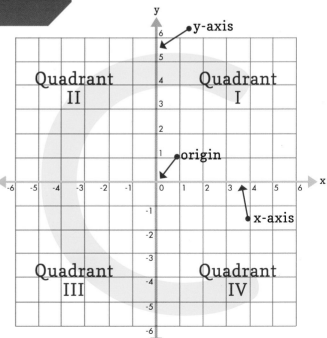

y

y-axis

6

5

Quadrant II

4

Quadrant I

3

2

origin

1

x

-6   -5   -4   -3   -2   -1   0   1   2   3   4   5   6

-1

x-axis

-2

-3

Quadrant III

-4

Quadrant IV

-5

-6

To plot an ordered pair, get a head start on the location by checking the x and y combination.

Quadrant	Positive or Negative x and y coordinates	Example
Quadrant I	x and y are both positive (+, +)	(6, 1)
Quadrant II	x is negative and y is positive (−, +)	(−3, 4)
Quadrant III	x and y are both negative (−, −)	(−5, −2)
Quadrant IV	x is positive and y is positive (+, −)	(4, −5)
No Quadrant	Any ordered pair containing a zero will lie directly on an axis.	(0, 0) (0, 3) (−1, 0)

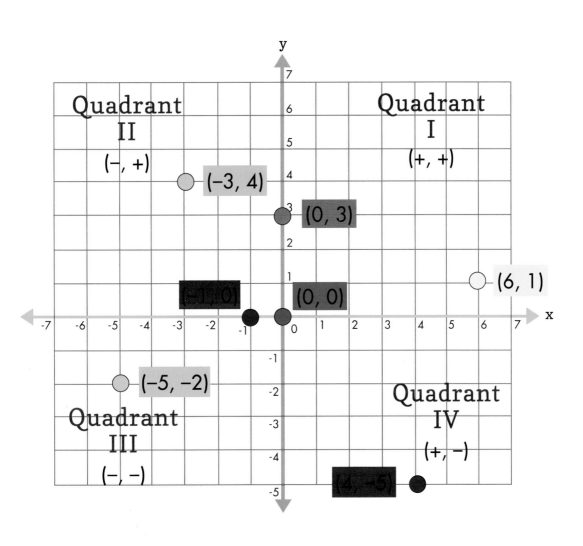

Glossary

absolute value (AB-suh-loot VAL-yoo): the distance between a number and zero on a number line

decimal (DESS-uh-muhl): a system of counting that is based on powers of ten

fraction (FRAK-shuhn): a number that is part of a group or part of a whole

inequality (in-i-KWOLL-uh-tee): symbols used to compare numbers and expressions

integer (IN-tuh-jur): whole numbers and their negative opposites

natural numbers (NACH-ur-uhl NUHM-burs): counting numbers beginning with 1, 2, 3

negative numbers (NEG-uh-tiv nuhm-burs): numbers less than zero

quadrant (KWAHD-ruhnt): the four areas created when the x-axis and y-axis intersect on a coordinate graph

rational numbers (RA-shun-nuhl NUHM-burs): numbers that are expressed as a quotient of two integers

Roman Numerals (ROH-man NOO-mur-uhlz): ancient Roman letters that represented numbers

whole numbers (HOLE NUHM-burs): counting numbers beginning with zero

Index

Websites to Visit

www.bbc.co.uk/bitesize/ks2/maths/number/negative_numbers/play

www.mathplayground.com/ASB_SpiderMatchIntegers.html

www.mathplayground.com/ASB_IntegerWarp.html

About the Author

Lisa Arias is a math teacher who lives in Tampa, Florida with her husband and two children. Her out-of-the-box thinking and love for math guided her toward becoming an author. She enjoys playing board games and spending time with family and friends.

Meet The Author!
www.meetREMauthors.com

PHOTO CREDITS: Cover: © Francey, Zentilia; Page 6: © Alvin Teo, Brian McEntire, DNY59; Page 10: © Pidjoe, Ashrafov, GoodOlga, arquiplay77, vm, Juan Monino; Page 11: © jpbcpa, ssuni, YinYang, eng3D

Edited by: Jill Sherman

Cover and Interior design by: Tara Raymo

Library of Congress PCN Data

Positive and Negative Numbers, Oh My!: Number Lines / Lisa Arias
(Got Math!)
ISBN 978-1-62717-719-1 (hard cover)
ISBN 978-1-62717-841-9 (soft cover)
ISBN 978-1-62717-954-6 (e-Book)
Library of Congress Control Number: 2014935599

Printed in the United States of America, North Mankato, Minnesota

Also Available as: